BOSTON MARRIAGE

BY DAVID MAMET

★

★

DRAMATISTS
PLAY SERVICE
INC.

2

This play is dedicated to Brigitte Lacombe.

BOSTON MARRIAGE was originally produced by the American Repertory Theatre (Robert Brustein, Artistic Director; Robert J. Orchard, Managing Director) at the Hasty Pudding Theatre in Cambridge, Massachusetts, on June 4, 1999. It was directed by David Mamet; the set design was by Sharon Kaitz and J. Michael Griggs; the lighting design was by John Ambrosone; and the costume design was by Harriet Voyt. The cast was as follows:

CLAIRE .... Rebecca Pidgeon
ANNA .... Felicity Huffman
CATHERINE .... Mary McCann

BOSTON MARRIAGE was subsequently produced by The Public Theater/New York Shakespeare Festival (George C. Wolfe, Producer; Mara Manus, Executive Director) in New York City on November 20, 2002. It was directed by Karen Kohlhaas; the set design was by Walt Spangler; the lighting design was by Robert Perry; the costume design was by Paul Tazewell; the wig and hair design were by Paul Huntley; and the production stage manager was James Latus. The cast was as follows:

CLAIRE .... Martha Plimpton
ANNA .... Kate Burton
CATHERINE .... Arden Myrin

CHARACTERS

ANNA and CLAIRE, two women of fashion

CATHERINE, the maid

PLACE

A drawing room.

BOSTON MARRIAGE

ACT ONE

A drawing room. Anna is seated in a day dress. She wears a large emerald necklace. Claire enters.

CLAIRE. I beg your pardon. Have I the right house?

ANNA. What address did you wish?

CLAIRE. Two forty-five.

ANNA. The number is correct in all particulars.

CLAIRE. Then it is the décor which baffles me.

ANNA. Have you not heard that this one or that, in an idle moment, conceives the idea to redecorate?

CLAIRE. Yes.

ANNA. You have heard?

CLAIRE. Indeed. But how does this inspired person pay for it?

ANNA. He tempers the wind to the shorn lamb.

CLAIRE. Who would that be?

ANNA. It is in the Bible.

CLAIRE. And has he an agent on the Earth, GOOD GOD, what is that around your neck?

ANNA. It is a necklace.

CLAIRE. … Oh, my Lord …

ANNA. What?

CLAIRE. Do you not find it … somewhat excessive for the morning?

ANNA. I wear it, should I be summoned on the instant, to choke

7

a horse.

CLAIRE. To choke a horse. Are not there men employed precisely for that purpose?

ANNA. Oh, dear, I should hate to think I was depriving them of livelihood.

CLAIRE. How good you are.

ANNA. Not at all.

CLAIRE. Might I be forgiven to ask: Is it Real?

ANNA. My dear, I have not lost my Taste …

CLAIRE. Then you have lost your virtue…?

ANNA. Yes.

CLAIRE. Thank God.

ANNA. A man gave it to me.

CLAIRE. A man.

ANNA. They do have such hopes for the mercantile.

CLAIRE. And those hopes so rarely disappointed.

ANNA. Well, we do love shiny things.

CLAIRE. In unity with our sisters the Fish.

ANNA. Men …

CLAIRE. What can one do with them.

ANNA. Just the One Thing.

CLAIRE. Though, in your case, it seems to've been effective.

ANNA. In like a Lion, out like a Lamb. *(Pause.)*

CLAIRE. This feller fancies you dead rotten.

ANNA. You don't know the *fraction* of it.

CLAIRE. Enlighten me.

ANNA. The Jewel.

CLAIRE. Yes.

ANNA. Not only is it *real:* it is a Family Heirloom.

CLAIRE. An Heirloom. How better-than-good!

ANNA. Been in his family five generations.

CLAIRE. O finders keepers. Well done!

ANNA. Only conceive, I pray you, that the Jewel is real, my debts are cleared, I have an account at the dressmaker's, and he has settled upon me, into the bargain, a monthly *stipend* …

CLAIRE. *Stop* …

ANNA. I tell you yes. Sufficient to support both me *and* you in Comfort.

CLAIRE. Oh bravo. For how glad one is. To see one's friend, come at long last into Safe Harbor.

ANNA. Thank you.

CLAIRE. Good for you, good for the side. But …

ANNA. Speak.

CLAIRE. This "man."

ANNA. Yes.

CLAIRE. This, this, this …

ANNA. My "Protector."

CLAIRE. Does he not know … does he not know your "reputation"?

ANNA. He is just returned from a long sojourn abroad.

CLAIRE. What? On the Moon?

ANNA. Ha ha.

CLAIRE. Is he in commerce on the Moon?

ANNA. … Ha.

CLAIRE. Is he a Dealer in Green Cheese? Is that your News? Have you beguiled a dairy man?

ANNA. I do not know his profession, or if, indeed, he follows one; I know that he is very rich. That he has been abroad, and that he, willy-nilly, delights in regaling me with various kickshaws significant of the esteem in which he holds me.

CLAIRE. … May it continue.

ANNA. How could it miscarry?

CLAIRE. Do not tempt fate.

ANNA. He worships me. What could go awry?

CLAIRE. Has he, for example, a wife?

ANNA. Why would he require a mistress if he had no wife? Of course he has a wife. But does this "wife" hold his affection? Does she wear This Jewel, magnificently wrought, unique in all the world?

CLAIRE. I must say that it suits you.

ANNA. I am told some ancestor once staked it against a half province in the Punjab.

CLAIRE. At what contest?

ANNA. … Could it have been *croquet?*

CLAIRE. … My golly they played high.

ANNA. But what *are* riches, whose reflections shine so cold …

CLAIRE. … Mmm …

ANNA. … In contrast with that true warmth, that sole, true

warmth, of Love and Friendship?

CLAIRE. That warmth incalculable and unvarying.

ANNA. Is it not so?

CLAIRE. Which delights in the success of the other.

ANNA. Aha, aha. I beg your pardon. For do I not perceive in you that roseate glow, my angel, my dove, and words of that character, which must speak of *your* triumph? Yes, I see that you have brought me a *bonne bouche* to console me for your so cruel and prolonged absence.

CLAIRE. You read my story in my face.

ANNA. When could I not? *How* I have missed you.

CLAIRE. One must follow the buffalo herd.

ANNA. And now you return, with news. You return, not unlike Prometheus. Who brought fire to the gods.

CLAIRE. The classical construction, of course, had him steal fire from the gods.

ANNA. He stole fire *from* the gods?

CLAIRE. Yes.

ANNA. And this is generally known.

CLAIRE. It is proverbial.

ANNA. I speak under correction.

CLAIRE. Might I have a cup of tea?

ANNA. Yes, yes, but with no further delay, now *your* news. Inform me. *(The maid enters.)*

MAID. Morning, miss.

ANNA. *(To Claire.)* Have you unearthed your *own* protector? Is *that* your report of the World's New Jest? What do you think, tea, Bridey, eh? Celebratory tea, and, in fact, we shall have a *party.* That's what we shall do. We shall have …

CLAIRE. Yes, curiously, that is *not* my news.

MAID. It's Catherine, miss.

ANNA. Yes, we shall have a party, and display through both my ostentation and my taste, the esteem …

MAID. It's Catherine, miss …

ANNA. … Excuse me … in which I hold you, My Dear Claire. Your place in my heart, and in my home. For what is home without you? A sounding brass or a tinkling cymbal.

CLAIRE. That is so well said …

10

ANNA. It is not mine.

CLAIRE. Its employment, however, is so touching.

ANNA. You spoil me.

CLAIRE. I speak but the truth.

ANNA. We shall have cakes and sweetmeats. The piquant and the sweet. Which only a sense of propriety debars me from conflating with my feelings. For *you,* my et cetera. How I have missed you.

CLAIRE. ... Bless you.

ANNA. Tea, Bridey, do you see? Pen and paper, for we are going to plan a fete ...

MAID. It's Catherine, miss ...

ANNA. And shall we invite, do I see in your eyes, a "Guest of Honor"? Some gentleman, perhaps, whom you have "brought to heel"? Is that your news? Tea, Bridey.

CLAIRE. No, that is not my news.

MAID. ... It's Catherine, miss.

CLAIRE. I am in Love.

ANNA. What did you say?

MAID. I said it's Catherine ... *(Pause.)*

ANNA. Not *Mary? (Pause.)* Not "Mary," I said? Or "Peggy"? *(Pause.)* Cringing Irish Terror, is it? What do you want? Home Rule, and all small children to raise geese? O ... Ireland, each and all descended from kings who strode five miles of lighted streets in Liffey whilst the English dwelt in caves. Is that the general tone of your Irish divertimento? *(Pause.)* Eh?

MAID. I'm Scottish, miss. *(Pause.)*

ANNA. Are you? *(Pause.)* I asked you a question.

MAID. Yes, miss.

ANNA. What is the main street in Edinburgh?

MAID. I don't know, miss.

ANNA. Where are you from?

MAID. From the Islands.

ANNA. What islands might those be?

MAID. The Orkney Islands, miss.

ANNA. Where are they situated? *(Pause.)*

CLAIRE. Where *are* they?

MAID. They are in the North, miss.

ANNA. In the North.

MAID. Yes.

ANNA. In the North of Scotland. *(Pause.)*

MAID. Yes. *(Pause.)*

ANNA. What *water* are they in?

MAID. … What water?

ANNA. Yes.

MAID. *(Pause.)* In the *sea,* miss.

ANNA. What's the name of it?

MAID. The name of the sea, miss?

ANNA. Yes. *(Pause.)*

MAID. The North Sea, miss.

ANNA. *(Pause. To Claire.) Dissolve … (Maid exits.)* Is it the North Sea, then?

CLAIRE. I believe it is.

ANNA. Is it?

CLAIRE. I think it is. *(Pause.)*

ANNA. Is it invariably called that?

CLAIRE. I believe so.

ANNA. Is it the sea we are wont to call the German Sea?

CLAIRE. The German Sea.

ANNA. Is it the same?

CLAIRE. I fear that there I disappoint you. *(Doorbell. The maid enters. Pause.)*

ANNA. What brings you back?

MAID. I've come to clear, miss.

ANNA. Why would you assume that service required? Has it not been but these two moments you have left the sweetmeats here? Is this some gastronomic monomania of yours? Some distaste for letting food "sit"? One would have thought to've encountered such in the Southern lands, where heat, engendering maggots, must inspire haste; from which, here in the North, the cold would have been supposed to've offered some protection.

CLAIRE. Your mistress suggests you needn't come until she's called you.

MAID. She did call me.

ANNA. To the contrary.

MAID. You rang the bell.

ANNA. Thank you, I haven't rung the bell. I haven't got a bell.

12

D'you see?

MAID. I heard a bell.

ANNA. Well, it is the front door, then. Why don't you answer it? *(Maid exits.)* And now, perhaps, to save my worthless life, you'd explain your late announcement. Pray let me but bind myself to the mast. *(The maid passes, in the BG.)* Who is it?

MAID. Fella come about the stove.

ANNA. Yes. What about the stove?

MAID. He came to fix it.

ANNA. Is it broken?

MAID. Yes, mum. *(Exits.)*

ANNA. Oh good. *(Pause.)* How do you find the weather? *(Pause.)* Do you not find it is fine?

CLAIRE. I find that it is *seasonable* ...

ANNA. ... Yes ...

CLAIRE. ... For this time of *year.*

ANNA. Mmm.

CLAIRE. And that is as far as I'm prepared to commit myself. *(Pause.)* But I was saying ...

ANNA. Yes, you were saying that you were "in Love." As you phrased it. You were, in midcareer, as it were, prating of this "Love."

CLAIRE. And you, friend of my Youth ...

ANNA. ... What memory ...

CLAIRE. At the announcement ...

ANNA. Yes?

CLAIRE. At the announcement, grow if I do not mistake, *cold.* Can you say why?

ANNA. *Why?*

CLAIRE. Yes.

ANNA. I have redecorated our room in chintz. In *chintz,* a fabric I abhor, in your absence, do you see? To please you.

CLAIRE. In chintz?

ANNA. You once expressed a preference for chintz.

CLAIRE. I?

ANNA. For *chintz,* which I have, oblivious to the verdict of the world, *festooned* ...

CLAIRE. I ...

13

ANNA. I come into funds, I come into funds, and my FIRST THOUGHT, do you see? Is it for myself? It is for *you*. Do I expect thanks? I would be glad of mute appreciation. I receive nothing but the tale of your new rutting. *(Pause.)* Oh how lonely you make me feel. How small. For how can one cherish, nay, how can one respect one, however dear, however well-formed, who acts so arbitrarily — so cruel? But yes, the engine of the world's betrayal, is it not? And we are sentenced to strive with the world. *(Pause.)*

CLAIRE. I'm sorry, what? *(Pause.)* Did I miss anything? *(Pause.)*

ANNA. I poured out my heart blood.

CLAIRE. Oh … *(Pause.)* I've forgotten what I was going to say.

ANNA. Say something *else*. *(Pause.)*

CLAIRE. How *practical* you are.

ANNA. For what *is* speech?

CLAIRE. I had often thought, it is as the chirping of the birds, minus their laudable disinterestedness.

ANNA. Oh what a vast, oh what a vast and pointless shithole it all is.

CLAIRE. What would that be?

ANNA. Our lives. *(Maid enters.)* What is it? What do you want? Saving national sovereignty and reparations? What? An apology for your potato famine? IT CAME FROM THE LACK OF ROTATION OF CROPS! Do you hear? From a depletion of…

CLAIRE. Nitrogen.

ANNA. Nitrogen, or something, in the soil. Do you think that the soil can go on forever, giving? *Giving.* Never a thought for replenishment? *Dirt,* do you see? Like every other thing in this green and confusing world, needs conservation and care, no less, in the end, than you and I. It is a thoughtless and, worse, unobservant soul who would say otherwise.

MAID. Mum.

ANNA. But you have my ear.

MAID. The dinner, mum.

ANNA. One would've thought that to've been the province of the cook. *(Pause.)* Oh, no.

CLAIRE. You never could keep help.

ANNA. Did she say it was because of the stove?

MAID. She did allow as how she couldn't cook with no stove.

14

CLAIRE. Well, one must credit her argument.

ANNA. Your attitude smacks of the republican.

CLAIRE. You flatter me.

ANNA. Plead with the cook to stay. *(Maid exits.)* But perhaps it is not love.

CLAIRE. It is love.

ANNA. But perhaps it is not.

CLAIRE. Then what would it be?

ANNA. You know, so many of our ills proceed from a corporeal imbalance.

CLAIRE. Do they?

ANNA. I tell you that they do.

CLAIRE. How lovely for them. To have, as it were, a provenance. In this gale of uncertainty.

ANNA. Mmm.

CLAIRE. To say, "I was engendered," for example, "by an excess of protein."

ANNA. 'S were we all, s'far as *that* goes ...

CLAIRE. Ah, yes, your newfound expertise.

MAID. *(Reentering.)* Cook's gone.

ANNA. Did you not plead with her?

MAID. Yes, miss.

ANNA. What did she say?

MAID. She said as how you could kiss her arse. Till ...

ANNA. Yes.

MAID. She said some holiday, but I've forgot it.

CLAIRE. Mayhap it will come to you.

MAID. God willing. You know, me Auld Gran used to say...

ANNA. *(To the maid.)* Oh, go away. *(Maid exits.)* And now we shall have no party; but of course now we have no cause.

CLAIRE. Oh, my dear.

ANNA. Escoffier had it as the last of the pleasures. Which will persist when all the rest have gone.

CLAIRE. When all the rest have gone.

ANNA. Yes.

CLAIRE. Escoffier did.

ANNA. Yes. *(Pause.)*

CLAIRE. Is it a word one may say in a drawing room?

ANNA. It is Food.

CLAIRE. *(Pause.)* Food.

ANNA. Yes.

CLAIRE. Food is the pleasure which persists. When all the rest have gone.

ANNA. According to Escoffier.

CLAIRE. *(Pause.)* And who was he?

ANNA. A cook.

CLAIRE. Well, it would be striking, then, had he said *otherwise.*

ANNA. Mmm. *(Pause.)* What didja *think* he meant?

CLAIRE. Oh, *you* know …

ANNA. Can you not conceive of a World Above your Waist?

CLAIRE. And *you:*

ANNA. Speak:

CLAIRE. I come, do you see, I come to you, with my *report* …

ANNA. … yes …

CLAIRE. Of that which I could neither *control* …

ANNA. … I take it you are speaking of your loins …

CLAIRE. Nor … ain't *you* an evil old bitch.

ANNA. I am not old.

CLAIRE. Older than I …

ANNA. Hardly true.

CLAIRE. What? Have they repealed the *calendar* …

ANNA. If it were true, it would be cruel to suggest it. You are cruel.

CLAIRE. Am I indeed.

ANNA. Yes. You are.

CLAIRE. I have a boon to beg.

ANNA. Oh what a shithole is the world, and how the friends of youth turn, until time, in its glass, seems to denounce one, and for what enormity? For primogeniture. Oh Lord, who seest all, I need a cup of tea. *(Pause.)* Mary. Mary!

CLAIRE. I'll tell you what you require. An electric bell.

ANNA. No. I think I would rather be tied to a cannon. I wish that I were dead. *(Pause.)* Why don't you leave? Your errand done, pray, take your congé — you have broke my heart.

CLAIRE. I have to ask a favor.

ANNA. Well, there is a time for everything. *(Pause.)* Except, of course, those things one has not time for. And what is there to be

16

done about *that? (Pause.)*

CLAIRE. Can I not induce you to share my ...

ANNA. ... No.

CLAIRE. Or, fine, then, to *endorse* ...

ANNA. I don't think so.

CLAIRE. My happiness.

ANNA. No. I don't see it happening.

CLAIRE. I cannot...?

ANNA. No. It's just not being done.

CLAIRE. Aha.

ANNA. And why should you require my endorsement? Why, for all that, would you, in the state of, this supposed state of, what?

CLAIRE. Bliss.

ANNA. Require of me anything at all? Would not a traditional understanding of the term "bliss" render its meaning "requiring nothing further of the world"?

CLAIRE. Do you know why I particularly hate it when my teeth begin to chatter?

ANNA. Why is that?

CLAIRE. Because they so seldom have anything to say.

ANNA. Aha. How *bold* it is. How courageous. Rich in that new-found courage. In the light of the New Thing. *(Pause.)* Love: which, which like religion, and the sea, which, like expensive jewelry, conquers all. *(Pause.)* 'Zat the thing?

CLAIRE. Yes.

ANNA. God forgive you.

CLAIRE. What am I to do?

ANNA. ... What is the problem? You told me, but I forgot.

CLAIRE. I am in *Love.*

ANNA. "Love."

CLAIRE. It is a state sung by the poets.

ANNA. So is death. But I don't see you floating in here and proclaiming, "I'm dead!"

CLAIRE. ... Aha.

ANNA. "I'm dead! I have *died! Embrace* me!" How wonderful for you. Many fine *people* are dead.

CLAIRE. How ill your disordered state becomes you.

ANNA. Tell it to the Marines.

17

CLAIRE. How I preferred my Friend of Old.

ANNA. Izzat so.

CLAIRE. Yes. Full of self-respect, inspiring …

ANNA. And who is the favored one?

CLAIRE. … Awe. Yes, awe, and, more to the point, emulation. In all who beheld her. Her *calm,* her …

ANNA. And what am I to do for a friend?

CLAIRE. No, I will always be your friend.

ANNA. Oh, faugh, you'll …

CLAIRE. I'll always …

ANNA. … Until the virus relents, you will be but the most abject boor, fit only to attempt to give or receive sensual satisfaction.

CLAIRE. I warrant you that I will always put my, my affection for you …

ANNA. … There was a time you would have said "love" …

CLAIRE. … And my regard for your interests, and your peace of mind …

ANNA. … You've ruined my life.

CLAIRE. Before everything.

ANNA. Liar, liar, liar.

CLAIRE. Saving, of course …

ANNA. Say "equal with."

CLAIRE. … I cannot.

ANNA. Say equal with.

CLAIRE. I …

ANNA. … those of my beloved.

CLAIRE. I …

ANNA. Say it, goddamnit to hell.

CLAIRE. I cannot.

ANNA. Say …

CLAIRE. It is impossible.

ANNA. Did I say "mean it"? Did I say "abjure hypocrisy"? You tell me you have some residual regard for me. I say, that being so, *lie.* You reply that you cannot. Burn in the vile circle of hell reserved for the virtuous and weak.

CLAIRE. I …

ANNA. And be damned. Go, and indulge yourself. With the object of your "love."

CLAIRE. You don't mean it?

ANNA. Sate yourself, till you are sick of love, then sate yourself with apples, then return to me bloated with roughage, distended …

CLAIRE. I …

ANNA. *Go* to your, your …

CLAIRE. … I have asked her to come here. *(Pause.)*

ANNA. You've asked her to come here. Your friend.

CLAIRE. Yes.

ANNA. For, for a vile "assignation."

CLAIRE. *(Pause.)* Yes.

ANNA. And what is your "boon"? My permission?

CLAIRE. I …

ANNA. Have you taken a vow of *arrogance?*

CLAIRE. … I am in love, I …

ANNA. Yes, so I understood you to have said. It is "love," you said that it was "love," did you not?

CLAIRE. It is love.

ANNA. And you have, therefore, presumed upon my, my, my, my …

CLAIRE. Your universally known and lauded generosity.

ANNA. But what is Love?

CLAIRE. … What is Love?

ANNA. That we should pine for it.

CLAIRE. No, no, I understood that to be your meaning. I require a place. I need a place, at which my friend and I…

ANNA. Your own home being? What? Too far? Too cold? Tainted by a life of depravity?

CLAIRE. I need a home where I may, with impunity …

ANNA. … Mmm?

CLAIRE. Take a … take a young …

ANNA. How young?

CLAIRE. Take a …

ANNA. You want me to be your beard.

CLAIRE. In short.

ANNA. You wish me to clothe your nakedness.

CLAIRE. I come to you, as I confess myself, as I beseech you, beyond shame.

ANNA. And this "shame," this "shame" you treasure, restores balance

19

to the world; this "shame," in whose Fine Light, all is permissible.

CLAIRE. I have no merit, to plead my case, but her *mother* ... to whom she is devoted. Do you see? To whom she is, unfortunately, tied. Her *mother* ...

ANNA. What about her mother? *(Pause.)*

CLAIRE. Well, the young thing cannot travel un*chaperoned,* her mother, who, mistakenly, takes on herself the child's supervision.

ANNA. How old *is* she?

CLAIRE. How old *is* who?

ANNA. Your friend. *(Pause.) I* see. And, so having delighted to pollute any residue of your own *reputation,* you make bold to squander mine.

CLAIRE. Please.

ANNA. And you *demean* me by the blithe assumption, that I would consent.

CLAIRE. I ...

ANNA. That I would Taint, that I would *endanger,* my, my compact with my New Protector ... Yes. My *Protector,* who provides the very *cushions* upon which we sit. *(Pause.)*

CLAIRE. To Market, to Market, to Be a Fat Pig. . .

ANNA. I did it for *you,* you ill-conditioned sow. I did it for the *cause.* He is a "man." What possible joy or diversion for *me* in this arrangement? I did it for *us,* for that unity-of-two which ... *(Crash in the kitchen.)*

CLAIRE. Ah, yes. The disruption of the Lowly, mimicking that of the Great.

ANNA. Perhaps *she's* in love. *(Maid enters.)*

MAID. I'm sorry, mum.

ANNA. Go away.

MAID. I'm sorry, I ...

ANNA. Retire.

MAID. I dropped the platter.

ANNA. Go away. Are you deaf? *(Pause.)* Say: Are you deaf? From the incessant roaring of the surf upon your savage, native shore? *(Pause.)* Go away. You stink of peat smoke.

MAID. We had a coal fire, miss.

ANNA. And what did you do? *Worship* it? *(Pause.)*

MAID. We lit it.

ANNA. *Did* you.

MAID. Yes, mum.

ANNA. What? To keep you Warm? *(Pause.)* Mmm? In the interminable nights when you lay there, bundled with your livestock, into the one room? Mmm? Whilst the savage and uncaring moon beat down, and so forth, engend'ring dreams of your escape to the Metropolis, thither to torment me? Is that what brings you here? After we've beseeched you to die?

MAID. I'm sorry that I dropped the plate, miss.

ANNA. Ah, yes, *that* was the import of the sound.

MAID. You c'n deduct it from my wages.

ANNA. And live in luxury the rest of my days. Oh good.

MAID. ... And ... and ... *(Dissolves in tears.)*

CLAIRE. Oh, *now* look what you've done. You never could deal with servants. Let me amend it. *(They watch the maid cry for a while.)* What is it? You're with child, by the man who pledged to marry you, now you discovered he's a wife and babe at home? *(Pause.)* 'Zat it? Something like that? *(Pause.)* Mmm? You try ...

ANNA. Y'r Da is dying of the Black Lung from a life spent in the Collieries, 'n' you lack the four pence which could transport him to rest and renewed vigor? *(Pause.)* Which is it? *(Pause.)* *Choose.* *(The maid exits.)* And now the tea will remain cold. *(Pause.)* Quite cold. 'N' who have I to blame. But myself. And an impersonal, and thoughtless deity. *(Pause.)*

CLAIRE. Help me.

ANNA. You are without shame.

CLAIRE. I have confessed it.

ANNA. Ah, no love as foolish as an Old Woman's love. *(Pause.)* An Old Woman's love. A HAG, et cetera, shorn of all, save those last vestiges of beauty, those final shreds, not clothing, nay, but framing her horrible plain face and form; that crone, reduced to sophistry to lure the young and the beautiful into her sway. And this is what it comes to, at the cold-fag end. To sit in dead conversation with the Duenna, to offer "cookies" to the chaperone, while you, and your young ... no, the mind cannot compass it. Oh what a constantly disrupted ... Oh what a disorderly ... Oh what a sad thing. The endless capacity of the world to unseat and disappoint us. Do you believe in God?

CLAIRE. I would if you'd shut up.

ANNA. And do you begrudge me my "keening"?

CLAIRE. Oh, pull your socks up.

ANNA. … I …

CLAIRE. Every note you strike is false. I cannot assemble them into a rational composition. You're like a spinet so bad out of tune the name of any note is arbitrary. How can one respect you? *(Pause.)*

ANNA. I beg your pardon.

CLAIRE. And I am sorry I was moved to speak with enthusiasm.

ANNA. I have forgotten it.

CLAIRE. Bless you.

ANNA. *(Pause.)* Sherry?

CLAIRE. Perhaps just a touch.

ANNA. … And you would have this young person come to my home.

CLAIRE. Yes.

ANNA. When?

CLAIRE. Today.

ANNA. You presume much. Yes — even now, I see you scour the street. This is the new thing, then. This is that for which it has amused God to spare me. *(Pause.)* Fine.

CLAIRE. … I beg your pardon?

ANNA. Have her come. *(Pause.)*

CLAIRE. You don't mean it.

ANNA. I shall grant graciously what I dare not refuse.

CLAIRE. Bless you, Oh Best of Friends.

ANNA. Is it not so?

CLAIRE. It *is* so. It *is* so.

ANNA. Godspeed you, and your Young Friend, to your Hour of Bliss.

CLAIRE. And God preserve you …

ANNA. Joy to your sheets.

CLAIRE. And may heaven both witness and endorse your sainted humanity.

ANNA. … Please … *(They drink.)* But may I, whilst preserving that essential veil of "decency"…

CLAIRE. Yes.

ANNA. Inquire …

CLAIRE. ... Please?

ANNA. *(Pause.)* That is, you take my meaning, "does" she, or ... to put it differently, "have" you ... *(Pause.)*

CLAIRE. She does not. We have not.

ANNA. Yes. Then, I have my own request.

CLAIRE. Anything under heaven.

ANNA. To, let us say, to, to *participate,* in ...

CLAIRE. I fear that my *vision of* the meeting ...

ANNA. Yes.

CLAIRE. Of the "geometry" of the thing ...

ANNA. Quite, no, you mistake me. I only meant to the extent that I ... set the *scene, ease* the transition, as it were: I, I bring you *cocoa,* I open the windows, and suggest you two would be more "cozy," underneath a "throw," I ...

CLAIRE. Yes, thank you, but ...

ANNA. Do you see? In the capacity of a *stage* manager, or ...

CLAIRE. I ...

ANNA. Yes, this shall be our party. And we must have a pie. Stress cannot exist in the presence of a pie.

CLAIRE. A pie.

ANNA. It casts out stress as the heat of the hand repels quicksilver. Faugh I say. Faugh. Keep you your precious vapors, your fantods, your anxiety. Give me a pie. Give me a pie *anyday.*

CLAIRE. Give me a pie, too. But ...

ANNA. For there is that of the bucolic in it. Is there not? The pie, the cottage, the ...

CLAIRE. The *hearth,* finally.

ANNA. Little Nell. Nell or Molly.

CLAIRE. Young ...

ANNA. That's right.

CLAIRE. Young Susan. Her brown arms shapely from the work of the fields. One wisp of her ...

ANNA. Dark blond hair.

CLAIRE. If you will, come down on her eyes. Brushed back with the flour-covered forearm. As she *kneads* the dough we may see the tendons now assemble now disperse beneath the nut-brown skin. She looks up. "I'm making a pie." *(Pause.)*

ANNA. Do you mock me?

CLAIRE. I am concocting a seduction. I do not require a *pâttissière*. *(Pause.)*

ANNA. What is there risible about a pie?

CLAIRE. Fine. And we must have ices.

ANNA. "Ices."

CLAIRE. I believe so. *(Pause.)*

ANNA. Ices.

CLAIRE. Yes.

ANNA. ... At a seduction?

CLAIRE. And, what, party favors, little, what are they? One gives them to the cook.

ANNA. Wallets.

CLAIRE. That's right. And the odd vial of scent.

ANNA. I just said "a pie."

CLAIRE. I riposted ices.

ANNA. ... But ...

CLAIRE. What is it you find abhorrent in them? Is it their, their artificial *color*, mmm? Or their *Frigidity* ... *(Pause.)*

ANNA. Oh. *(Pause.)*

CLAIRE. I beg you to accept my deep and unreserved apology, my tongue has run away with me. I have traduced both the memory of our friendship and the fact of our love. I am alone, in the midst of my own folly, of my need and vice. I stand naked before you, in my panting and unclean depravity, and beg for your aid. *Help* me.

ANNA. *(Pause.)* All right.

CLAIRE. Oh, Blessed forgiveness.

ANNA. But I want to watch.

CLAIRE. You whore.

ANNA. Not in the room. Not in the *room*. What do you take me for, my God.

CLAIRE. You Pagan slut.

ANNA. Through a *hole* in the wall.

CLAIRE. No.

ANNA. Did I say I want to *participate?* Or *Comment?*

CLAIRE. I said no.

ANNA. Or *advise,* which, given the *youth of* the ...

CLAIRE. I said no.

ANNA. ... might *not* be supererogatory.

CLAIRE. Rave on.

ANNA. Ah. Yes. Love. Love for thee, but not for *me. My* sacrifice is *naught*. While *you,* yes … *Gaze* through the window. Gaze in vain, while we may sit here and beguile the hour, in parsing the distinction between Friendship and Acquaintance. Lug your trick off to the park. Amuse the *nannies* with their *prams*. "What's that, nanny?" "Well, that's just two women, dear." "But, nanny, what are they *doing?*" Off you go.

CLAIRE. *(At the window.)* Oh my God. It is she. I recognize the conveyance.

ANNA. Oh your new friend. Is she come?

CLAIRE. She is here.

ANNA. Hard cheese.

CLAIRE. Oh, what is more foolish than the unrequited love of the old? *(Pause.)* I beg you …

ANNA. Ah.

CLAIRE. … If …

ANNA. No, no, it is not enough, my dear, to say, "I see the Penalty, pray do not tax yourself inflicting it."

CLAIRE. I beg your pardon. It is a sign of my distraction … I plead with you: anything within my power. I'd do it for you, you know I would. Were the situation reversed.

ANNA. But the situation, you will allow, *is not* reversed.

CLAIRE. Cold, heartless woman.

ANNA. Am I, indeed?

CLAIRE. Of whom they once said heart of bronze if any heart at all.

ANNA. Izzat what they once said?

CLAIRE. Once, yes, once we strove together.

ANNA. I do seem to remember.

CLAIRE. A small band of Freebooters, share alike …

ANNA. … yes, it was so …

CLAIRE. And now, as you've come into your Patrimony …

ANNA. Aha …

CLAIRE. You've found a *Protector.* And the Emerald round your Neck the ensign of that selfishness, that jealousy Engendered by Wealth …

ANNA. Aha.

CLAIRE. For it's riches that have sundered you.

ANNA. Is it indeed?

CLAIRE. You say Share Alike, and *I* say: your abode, for Part of One Day …

ANNA. Yes, it is not exactly the "use of the Hall," which …

CLAIRE. Cold, cold, ancient, jealous hag.

ANNA. I see you are disordered. Shall I loosen your stays?

MAID. *(Entering.)* There's a young person at the door.

ANNA. Yes. No, I'm not at all sure that I am "at home." Oh my. No, I am not at home. Pray, have her call again some other time.

CLAIRE. Yes. You shall set the scene. You shall set the scene and aid me, aid the two of us by the tone, by, by the gracious attentions …

ANNA. … That is all I asked.

CLAIRE. It shall be as you say.

ANNA. Then we may proceed. *(Exits.)*

MAID. Lovely day for it, miss. But I'd wear my hat.

CLAIRE. I *beg* your pardon.

MAID. 'F I went for a walk.

CLAIRE. Aha, yes, I mistook you.

MAID. What'd you *think* I meant?

CLAIRE. Nothing.

MAID. I wouldn't wear me hat in *bed* …

CLAIRE. … What reserve. *(Anna reenters.)*

ANNA. Yes, it seems it is your young friend. I must endorse your choice. Exquisite.

CLAIRE. And you will afford us privacy and shelter. For the afternoon.

ANNA. And participate …

CLAIRE. Within the limits of …

ANNA. … As agreed.

CLAIRE. And you swear to divert her chaperone?

ANNA. She has come alone.

CLAIRE. Oh, Joy.

ANNA. And we are agreed as to terms?

CLAIRE. We are. Urge her in. *(Claire nods. Anna walks to the doorway and addresses a person, off.)*

MAID. *(Off.)* Miss, I didn't catch yer name?

ANNA. *(Off.)* Welcome, yes, Welcome to my Abode. How good

of you to come, if you would be so kind as to, Bridey. Bridey. Would you please ... *(Anna reenters.)*

CLAIRE. If you'd excuse me ... *(Brushes past them.)*

MAID. It's Catherine, miss.

ANNA. Good lookin' little thing, eh?

MAID. I couldn't say, miss.

ANNA. No, indeed, she is. And you yourself, you know, you are not unattractive.

MAID. What, mum?

ANNA. Has no one told you that before?

MAID. No, mum.

ANNA. Aha. Do you garner the thrust of my declaration?

MAID. I think so, mum.

ANNA. But what, it repels you?

MAID. No, mum, but.

ANNA. Yes?

MAID. What would I tell me parents?

ANNA. That you had found a secure position.

MAID. May I think about it?

ANNA. Indeed.

MAID. Thank you, mum. *(Claire reenters.)*

CLAIRE. She is upset.

ANNA. Well, la! How that astonishes me. One must set the stage. Proceed with measure. And you will thank God that I am here to pace your advances.

CLAIRE. It is not my advances which upset her.

ANNA. Say, then.

CLAIRE. She asks me about *you.*

ANNA. About me — She is *jealous.* She is *jealous,* the dear thing.

CLAIRE. She is not jealous.

ANNA. Is she not, then what is it about me upsets her?

CLAIRE. She asks why you are wearing her mother's necklace.

ACT TWO

Scene 1

Somewhat later. The drawing room. Anna is seated alone. Catherine, the maid, enters.

ANNA. Someone was at the door?

MAID. Yes, miss.

ANNA. What was the message?

MAID. Message?

ANNA. Do not spare me. I am prepared.

MAID. There wuunt no message.

ANNA. Then who was at the door?

MAID. It was the fella 'bout the stove. He said …

ANNA. Has no one left a letter?

MAID. No, miss.

ANNA. Fell circumstance. Oh, how you chastise my presumption. I am undone. My protector will withdraw his stipend as my love, her love, and I shall starve, the hollow percussion of my purse, a descant to that of my broken heart. But once I was young and the world before me. And once men were other than the depraved swine time and experience have revealed them to be. Once the world was to me a magic place … I was a Little Girl, oh, once …

MAID. D'you mind if I work while you're talkin', miss? *(Pause.)* 'Ld it disturb you, like? You needn't think, like, that I'd evade yer privacy. *(Pause.)* 'Cause I can't, the life o'me, tell what the fuck yer on about. *(Pause.)*

ANNA. I was speaking of my shattered dreams.

MAID. Don't let me hinder ye.

ANNA. Most kind.

MAID. Because me Auld Gran used to say …

28

ANNA. Will you stuff a sock in it?

MAID. Yes, mum ...

ANNA. Has no one called?

MAID. Not to the best of my knowledge, no. *(Pause.)*

ANNA. Ah, then, good-bye to Comfort ...

MAID. ... Fella said that I bring it on myself.

ANNA. ... Goodbye to joy, and goodbye to my own lover for whom I strove to "feather our nest" ... That you bring what on yourself?

MAID. Criticism.

ANNA. I have no doubt that you do.

MAID. B'cause ...

ANNA. In fact, I've seen it demonstrated.

MAID. Because ... *(Dissolves crying.)*

ANNA. *What? (Pause.)* What? Are you crying?

MAID. No, miss.

ANNA. Have you no *sympathy,* I have lost my income, and I've alienated the affection of my one true love. What is your particular complaint? *(Maid sobs.)* Oh fine, fine. Go on. Heave your apron to your eyes.

MAID. It's too short, miss.

ANNA. Well, then, run in and *change. (Pause.)* Put on a longer apron.

MAID. They're in the wash.

ANNA. Well, you should have thought ahead. *(Maid cries.) What...?*

MAID. Miss, I'm that homesick, I swear, that I'd fuck the ragman just to hear a friendly word.

ANNA. Believe me, I know the feeling.

MAID. I'm sure you do.

ANNA. What *can* you mean...? *(Doorbell rings.)* Go. Get the door. *(Maid exits. Claire enters.)*

CLAIRE. What have you heard?

ANNA. Oh, thank God, you are returned.

CLAIRE. What have you heard?

ANNA. Thank God. I feared that I had alienated you.

CLAIRE. She has not...? She has not written.

ANNA. She ...

CLAIRE. My young friend.

ANNA. Oh.

CLAIRE. Has she?

ANNA. What could she write?

CLAIRE. She could write her love, could she not? Or she could write, oh God, she could write that we, though momentarily thwarted …

ANNA. I would say, my dear, that the communiqué which we have to *fear* is from her father.

CLAIRE. From her father.

ANNA. Wouldn't you say?

CLAIRE. From her *father?*

ANNA. He has been discovered in a malversation, do you see, of his wife's jewelry. And how was it discovered? His daughter came to a depraved and illicit assignation and spied it draped round the neck of her intended's tribad paramour.

CLAIRE. Have you taken up journalism?

ANNA. What a vile thing to say.

CLAIRE. You look like a dead cart horse.

ANNA. … Is that my muff?

CLAIRE. You gave it to me *years* ago. How Dare You … do you stoop to, to, to, to *attempt* to humble me, by calling up past favors?

ANNA. No.

CLAIRE. Then what was the import of your mention of the muff?

ANNA. I was surprised it had come back in style.

CLAIRE. God damn you to hell.

ANNA. I suppose if one waits long enough …

CLAIRE. You look like a plate of cold stew.

ANNA. I did not sleep last night.

CLAIRE. And I shall never sleep again. I shall stand vigil, my burning eyes fixed on eternity, awaiting that word which will never come.

ANNA. They *will* call, of course.

CLAIRE. Oh, do you think, oh, Good!

ANNA. They will call to demand the return of the necklace …

CLAIRE. To demand the necklace.

ANNA. For a certainty.

CLAIRE. Aha.

ANNA. I have it here. *(She takes out a small jewelry bag.)*

CLAIRE. How come you to act so Blithe?

ANNA. Why care I for the loss of a Jewel? Let him restore it, to his "wife," or ... *whatever* employee of his he has filched it from.

CLAIRE. And take with him, will he not, all your support, your equipage, your ...

ANNA. That must be as it will be.

CLAIRE. Do you not find such a disposition trivial?

ANNA. It is, as I understand the term, *Philosophy. (Pause.)* How can philosophy be trivial? When have you known me to be trivial?

CLAIRE. You once referred to the Crimean War as "just one of those Things."

ANNA. I did?

CLAIRE. Yes.

ANNA. When did I do that?

CLAIRE. During a discussion of Geopolitics.

ANNA. What is or are Geopolitics?

CLAIRE. Oh, *you* remember ...

ANNA. I do not.

CLAIRE. They are, as the term might suggest, the politics of the world.

ANNA. And why were we discussing them?

CLAIRE. To pass the time. To pass the time, you vacant cow. That is what people do. When they are thrust together. During *dinner,* or ...

ANNA. Yes ...

CLAIRE. Or, *marriage* ...

ANNA. Yes, you do fight shy of the domestic.

CLAIRE. *Do* I?

ANNA. I must say you do.

CLAIRE. Why would *that* be?

ANNA. It baffles me.

CLAIRE. Does it, indeed?

ANNA. Yes. Which situation has So Much to Offer.

CLAIRE. To "those of that bent." *(Doorbell rings. Pause. Rings again. Maid enters.)*

MAID. I'm goin' to get the door. *(Pause. Maid exits.)*

ANNA. Are you prepared?

CLAIRE. I am prepared.

ANNA. Oh, fate inexorable. Oh, fate misthought at first to be but circumstance, revealed at last as the minute operations of the gods. Oh fate but our own character congealed into a burning glass. Focus your cleansing light upon me, and I shall be cleansed.

CLAIRE. *(Mumbling.)* ... You *gave* me this goddamned muff ...

ANNA. *(Maid enters.)* Show them in.

MAID. Show who in? *(Pause.)*

ANNA. Who was at the door?

MAID. It was the stove mechanic. He said ...

ANNA. I don't care what he said.

CLAIRE. Why has he come again, if the stove is operational?

MAID. It ain't exactly operational.

CLAIRE. In what respects is it deficient?

MAID. You need some new parts. He ...

ANNA. Go away.

MAID. He ...

ANNA. You are unwanted. And the tea is cold.

MAID. ... Nothing the matter with cold tea ...

ANNA. ... I beg your pardon?

MAID. I've had worse, and so, I'd think, have you. No offense.

ANNA. "No offense"? You impertinent *cooze* ...

MAID. I only meant, in a long life, some point, it's likely come down to Short Rations. *(Pause.)*

ANNA. In a long life.

MAID. Yes, miss. *(Exits.)*

ANNA. Oh, how the Lesser Beasts draw strength, at the spectacle of the Lioness beset.

CLAIRE. ... Oh, God.

ANNA. And All is Confusion, at the Waterhole.

MAID. *(Reentering.)* Mum.

ANNA. Go away, or I'm going to have you killed.

CLAIRE. How would you go about it?

ANNA. Well, I'm sure that there are ways.

CLAIRE. You are?

ANNA. Of course. One reads of it all the time.

CLAIRE. Mmm?

ANNA. In the Papers? "Such and so, having engaged the services of an Assassin ... "

CLAIRE. Isn't that "having left my Bed and Board ... "
ANNA. You think with your loins.
CLAIRE. Oh, Land of Goshen. Oh, how more than droll. What of your Bible now? What of Forbearance, meek and mild ...
ANNA. ... Kiss my ass.
CLAIRE. Ho, but perhaps they'll come again. Perhaps my Love, and perhaps your Protector. Blind to your past, indifferent to your limitations, rich as Croesus. Perhaps they approach now. Yes, as all things can be mended by wishing; as the child, mangled by the cart, can be made whole by apology. You have fucked my life into a cocked hat. *(She begins to cry. Anna goes to her to comfort her.)*
ANNA. There, there ...
CLAIRE. Oh, thank you, I feel so much better. We shall end life together, old and friendless, desired by no one, devoid of all save memory, and these most wistful of words:
MAID. *(Entering.)* While I was admiring your muff, your parts came. *(Pause.)*
CLAIRE. I beg your pardon.
MAID. I was admiring your muff.
CLAIRE. It was a gift from a friend.
MAID. And while I was distracted, mum, yer parts came.
ANNA. My parts?
MAID. The parts for the stove.
ANNA. Thank you, that will be all. *(Maid exits. To Claire.)* Now, listen and be taught.
CLAIRE. No.
ANNA. I say Yes. I offer you the comforts of philosophy. Your little friend, your young friend, she was just a passing whim.
CLAIRE. And he was your last chance.
ANNA. Yes, that is cruel, but I forgive you. For we both have gone astray.
CLAIRE. You make me throw up.
ANNA. We've gone astray. We have become habituated to that vile weed, Luxury, which grows, in the night, like the *Ricinus* plant, in the Bible.
CLAIRE. The plant in the Bible.
ANNA. Yes.
CLAIRE. In the morning room?

33

ANNA. I beg your pardon?

CLAIRE. The one near the Ficus? Do you know, and here again, I always *told* you. You listen to nothing, my dear. You have a diverting and quixotic *view* of things, but you take advice from nothing that lives.

ANNA. What do you mean?

CLAIRE. I told you repeatedly it was too damp in there.

ANNA. In where?

CLAIRE. In the morning room.

ANNA. You never said anything remotely of the sort.

CLAIRE. I ruined a perfectly good, what do you mean I never said anything? I ruined my new black velvet *reticule*.

ANNA. ... If ...

CLAIRE. I, *excuse* me. In This House of Horrors. *That* night, we, but I see you have repressed it.

ANNA. ... Repressed *what?* ...

CLAIRE. ... And how *dare* you take refuge in the Bible?

ANNA. ... Many recur to it in times of Stress.

CLAIRE. ... What nonsense.

ANNA. Quite the contrary.

CLAIRE. You have ruined my life.

ANNA. Things Occur. Claire. I *pray* you, do not mope, and fret. Things occur. That is their nature. Do you see? Change ...

CLAIRE. Change.

ANNA. It is the nature of all things.

CLAIRE. *"Change"*...?

ANNA. Yes.

CLAIRE. Oh, how I loathe a poseur.

ANNA. Please?

CLAIRE. You mean to denigrate my loss, by your display of equanimity in the face of your own.

ANNA. *Have* I not undergone, you will forgive my ironic employment of the term "a reversal"?

CLAIRE. And what of my reticule?

ANNA. Bother your reticule. *(Pause.)* What reticule?

CLAIRE. ... We had met at a certain person's house, I see it clear as Arctic day, and you perceived such and such a one was forming, an attachment for me. And I repaired here, after the fete, with, as

I then thought, the best of boon companions, whereupon you jealously began to *sulk*. And I had laid my reticule upon the étagère, in the solarium, next to your dread ficus plant, which dripped upon my reticule and left it water-spotted and ruint. Then ...

ANNA. I stipulate to the tale's essential verity.

CLAIRE. ... You remember it?

ANNA. No, but I'd swear to heresies untold if you'd shut up. What is your point?

CLAIRE. That I'd informed you, at that time, that you maintained an overdank and fetid atmosphere in the solarium. It dropped on my reticule. And now it's rotted your Bible.

ANNA. Oh. Ha. Oh, ha. Oh ha ha ha ha ha.

CLAIRE. You have the advantage of me.

ANNA. It grows in the story of Jonah.

CLAIRE. What?

ANNA. The *Ricinus* plant.

CLAIRE. Of Jonah and the Whale.

ANNA. Yes. In the Bible.

CLAIRE. A plant.

ANNA. Yes. You unlettered spiv.

CLAIRE. Which has what reference for us?

ANNA. *I opined ...*

CLAIRE. Yes ...

ANNA. That I had grown inured to luxury. Until the increasing need of it, do you see?

CLAIRE. ... I am too ill for words.

ANNA. ... Where is your sense of humor?

CLAIRE. Where is *yours?*

ANNA. Oh la. Where could it be?

CLAIRE. Gone to Arcturus, with the rest of the light ...

ANNA. Where *is* Arcturus?

CLAIRE. In the Heavens.

ANNA. Is it a star?

CLAIRE. I would think so.

ANNA. Far far away?

CLAIRE. Of necessity.

ANNA. Lovers agog at the "immensity" of it all.

CLAIRE. ... Yes?

ANNA.   Good then, see here, the star. It's not *yours*. Do you know? It's not your soul. It's the sky. It sits there and displays this or that trick of the light, and your kidneys, or spleen, direct you to mate, and you gaze upward.

CLAIRE.   Mmm.

ANNA.   Because you are a *poet?* No. BECAUSE YOU ARE OUTSIDE. It would seem equally sublime, were you cased in a *piano* crate, squinting at the screws.

CLAIRE.   ... Indeed.

ANNA.   It is none other than our friend, the Mating Instinct.

CLAIRE.   Mmm.

ANNA.   Toying with you. Once again.

CLAIRE.   And what would you know of that? Greek to a Goose.

ANNA.   I pray you would indulge me for a space, for I am going to set out on a speech, which may have some duration, but whose theme may be gleaned from its opening phrase: HOW DARE YOU?

CLAIRE.   No. No. No. It is not *fair*. Do you see? It is not *fair*.

ANNA.   What is "fair"? Is Love Fair?

CLAIRE.   Mmm.

ANNA.   Is it fair, that the sea, for example, should rage wide and savage, erasing whole towns and coastal ...

CLAIRE.   Settlements?

ANNA.   No, well, yes, certainly, but I meant the ... the ... the sites of agriculture ... *(Pause.)*

CLAIRE.   "Farms"?

ANNA.   Thank you. Then retreat to that calm beauty so cherished by painters of the second class? *(Pause. Maid enters.)* Have they come? Have they called? What? Has a letter arrived?

MAID.   No, miss.

ANNA.   Well then, what brings you here? Sick Curiosity? Come for the Spectacle...? Oh, no. I see it: Years to come: our Martha here, back in Ireland, reinstalled by her Peat fire, the wee bairns, listening, once again, to Grandmother's saga, "My time in the City," listening, each for her favorite part, for one the splendor, for one the *scope* ...

CLAIRE.   ... For one the end.

ANNA.   In the so-heavy odor of the village bodies, in that "hut," where the very caulking, of the walls … What is it made of? What is it made of? The, the caulking …

CLAIRE. What's it made of?

MAID. Mud.

ANNA. "Miss."

MAID. Mud, miss.

CLAIRE. Of that river mud, so suggestive of sex to the preorgasmic mind, that mud …

MAID. Actually, they dig it from the barrow, miss.

CLAIRE. From the barrow.

MAID. From the hill. Me Auld Gran used to say …

CLAIRE. I know what a barrow is.

MAID. Yes, miss.

CLAIRE. *I wondered* that the *barrow* mud was *moist* enough. *(Pause.)* Of fog, sweat, peat smoke, and that ineffable *reek,* so redolent of … *childbirth,* copulation, of, of …

MAID. Actually, it isn't moist, miss. That's why it falls out. *(Pause.)* It dries up.

CLAIRE. It dries up.

MAID. The mud. *(Pause.)*

CLAIRE. What do they do then?

MAID. They, well. They moisten it, and they replace it.

ANNA. Whyn't they just use moister mud?

MAID. Well, I'm sure that they do, you see, but, but, but, but, that, as time goes by …

ANNA. Mmm-hmm.

MAID. … It all dries out. *(Pause.)*

CLAIRE. Aha.

MAID. However you moisten it. *(Starts to cry.)*

ANNA. Why are you crying?

MAID. 'Cause I'll have to leave.

ANNA. Have you been spying on your Betters?

CLAIRE. Eavesdropper.

ANNA. Is that the happy excuse for your visit? To profess your chagrin over our reversal?

MAID. Yes, that's right, miss. I came to see was there 'nything I c'ld do to *help.*

CLAIRE. Oh, Wizard! Brave Sorority indomitable. Come to support us in our grief. Yes. Boil Water. Make a poultice. *(Pause.)*

ANNA. What?

CLAIRE. What could you do to help?

MAID. I was goin' to say, that it's like *rowing.*

ANNA. *(Pause.)* What is like rowing?

MAID. The troubles between women and men.

CLAIRE. Pray. How is it like rowing?

MAID. Men have big shoulder blades. Our shoulder blades are smaller. Which means less power rowing. Although, if you row *correctly,* you should use yer *legs,* which, women, have big muscles in our *legs. (Pause.)* Though, of course, it don't make much difference in a *short* pull. *(Pause.)*

ANNA. What doesn't make a difference?

MAID. Rowing.

CLAIRE. Why does it make that much difference, then, rowing a long way?

MAID. Because, miss, like many things in life, a lack of form can be hid in the short run, its absence being taken up by *power. (Pause.)*

CLAIRE. How do you come to know so much about the nautical?

MAID. I was on a boat once.

CLAIRE. *Really.*

ANNA. That will be all. *(Maid exits. Pause.)*

CLAIRE. You were going to say something.

ANNA. What about?

CLAIRE. How the deuce should *I* know…? *(Pause.)*

ANNA. I've forgotten what I was going to say.

CLAIRE. Well, say something *else,* for the love of God. *(Maid enters.)*

MAID. Mum.

ANNA. Oh MIGHT YOU GET OFF MY TITS? What *is* it? *(Pause.)*

MAID. I've told a lie.

CLAIRE. Well, then you're going to hell.

ANNA. A lie about what?

MAID. I can't rightly say it.

ANNA. Oh, spit it out.

MAID. It's me's in trouble.

ANNA. Go on.

MAID. I've lost me most precious possession.

CLAIRE. Your Rapier Wit?

MAID. No.

CLAIRE. I give up. *(Pause.)*

MAID. Me *maidenhood.*

CLAIRE. How icky.

ANNA. When did it occur?

MAID. During before when you had yer tea.

ANNA. Aha.

MAID. No, not the *whole* of it.

ANNA. No.

MAID. ... Jus' between the first time that you rang for the Hot water.

ANNA. Mmm.

MAID. No, not even. No, I tell a lie. It was when I came back with the tray.

ANNA. Yes ...

MAID. But b'fore I put the tray down.

ANNA. Ah.

MAID. That's why the cook quit.

ANNA. Is it?

CLAIRE. ... Didn't like the entertainment?

MAID. No, I tell a lie. I'd put th' tray *down,* do you see, but I wz holdin' *on* to it, on to the handles, like, while it was on the counter.

CLAIRE. ... Thank you, yes.

MAID. ... For ...

CLAIRE. ... That's quite enough.

MAID. For "balance." *(Pause.)*

CLAIRE. Ah, yes.

MAID. And I'm afraid I've spilt the milk. *(Maid cries.)*

ANNA. Oh, Man — oh, Adversary Implacable. What does one not sacrifice upon the altar of your merciless caprice? *(To Maid.)* Go away. You're fired.

CLAIRE. Are you deaf? You're sacked. Go away now, go home.

MAID. I can't go home.

ANNA. Can't you see, we have troubles of our own?

CLAIRE. Have you no sympathy?

MAID. I can't go home, I'm *ruined.*

39

CLAIRE. You ain't ruined. Just don't *tell* nobody. You dense *cow.* Don't tell anyone. And pray to the gods your friend has neither given you the *pox,* or a *child. (Maid cries.)* Shall I write it *down* for you…?

ANNA. Go, go, go, go away, you sad, immoral harlot.

MAID. I don't know what to *do.*

CLAIRE. Well, what would your Auld Gran say?

MAID. I don't know.

CLAIRE. Well, go home and ask her.

MAID. She's dead.

CLAIRE. She should have taken better care of herself.

MAID. Waal, she lived a long life.

CLAIRE. Oh, good.

MAID. She was forty.

ANNA. … Aha …

MAID. But she always said, My Gran, she would Reach Out from Beyond the Grave.

CLAIRE. Told Fortunes, did she?

ANNA. Go away.

CLAIRE. Turned the odd trick? Fill up the Family Larder?

MAID. … She had the second sight.

CLAIRE. … How handy.

MAID. The islanders said she could see right through a man and two yards into the dirt that he stood on. One time, Annie MacPherson lost her locket. Actually, she lost it more than once. She never could hold on to anything. She used to tie her shovel to her apron strings when she went out to work in the garden. That's how she broke her ankle. One time, she baked a trowel in a pie. *(Pause.)* I must pull up me bootstraps. Yer right. I'll go.

CLAIRE. Oh top *hole! (Pause.)*

ANNA. Happy Day.

MAID. Because me Auld Gran used to say …

CLAIRE. Oh, for Christ's sake, let her void herself.

ANNA. What did your Auld Gran say?

MAID. "Life is Froth and Life is Bubble. Two things stand like stone. Kindness in another's trouble. Courage in your own." *(Pause. Maid exits.)*

CLAIRE. We've fallen victim to the worst sin.

ANNA. Farting in Church?

CLAIRE. Despair.

ANNA. … That is the worst sin?

CLAIRE. The girl is right.

ANNA. In what particular?

CLAIRE. Fine. We are mired in difficulties. We must extricate ourselves.

ANNA. I am all attention.

CLAIRE. Our fortunes are turned upon the unwonted discovery in your home of a specific emerald bauble.

ANNA. In brief.

CLAIRE. All, then, we must do is excuse its presence here.

ANNA. You bound before me.

CLAIRE. Look here. You are a jeweler. You are a lapidary. He brought the Emerald to you to have it Reset. *(Pause.)*

ANNA. No.

CLAIRE. You are a sleuth. You are a detectress. Commissioned to locate and restore the stolen necklace.

ANNA. … No …

CLAIRE. You are a valuer for an Assurance Firm.

ANNA. Hold *hard*. Hold *hard* … No no no no better than that. Better than that *far:* Do you see? You brought her to me. You brought the little twat here. You bought the trollop here to … *(Maid enters. Pause.)* What?

MAID. Are ye angry with me, mum?

ANNA. Do you know why you people perished? Do you know? In your precious potato famine? Do you think it was chance? You *died,* through a criminal lack of concern for the nitrogen content of the soil. *(Pause. Maid exits crying.)*

CLAIRE. Where were we?

ANNA. … It is gone.

CLAIRE. No, I deny it.

ANNA. It is vanished.

CLAIRE. *Best* of friends. Most inventive of Preceptors …

ANNA. You brought her here … *(Pause.)* No.

CLAIRE. How may I retrieve that Philosopher's stone, which bid fair to repair our fortunes? How can I jog your memory?

ANNA. No, it is gone.

CLAIRE. How may I recruit your dispersed fancies?

41

ANNA. Distract me.

CLAIRE. Uh, uh, uh … Once two little children went into the woods …

ANNA. No.

CLAIRE. All right, once upon a time … Once in the course of human events, wait: Awake! The roseate hue of dawn steals o'er the sleeping copse. Hark! Hark! The hunting horn … something … something … "Foxes" …

ANNA. Yes. Yes. I have it.

CLAIRE. " … Little kit fox, why weep'st thou? For, though your daddy dies, he gives healthy amusement to the county" … Uh … "Let *us,* then, like that dying fox, discern *our* place in life, and … " *(Pause.)* "And … "

ANNA. Have you run down?

CLAIRE. I seem to.

ANNA. Good. I have the Perfect Plan.

CLAIRE. I beg your pardon — Disgorge it.

ANNA. Upon the one proviso.

CLAIRE. … a proviso?

ANNA. That should I resurrect our Fortunes, you swear to see this twit no more.

CLAIRE. You swine.

ANNA. Everything has a price.

CLAIRE. You Visigoth.

ANNA. And having a price, has a price tag, read it.

CLAIRE. I shall see her the once.

ANNA. Granted.

CLAIRE. In privacy.

ANNA. For how long?

CLAIRE. An afternoon.

ANNA. Done.

CLAIRE. You concede so blithely. Why?

ANNA. And she unbroken to the Bit? All innocent of the Chafe of the Saddle … And Shy of the Touch of Man. Progress how you will, I feel the one afternoon will hardly avail you.

CLAIRE. That will be as it may.

ANNA. And I want to watch.

CLAIRE. Outside of the room.

ANNA. I'll fetch the auger.

CLAIRE. Tell me the plan.

ANNA. You tell the girl that her father came, to visit a Famous Clairvoyant …

CLAIRE. Mmm.

ANNA. Madame de …

CLAIRE. No, I get ya …

ANNA. And he brought her mother's Jewel …

CLAIRE. Say on …

ANNA. In order to divine by it. *(Pause.)* Whdja Think?

CLAIRE. It is the least credible explanation of Human Behavior I have ever heard.

ANNA. Of course. But you miss the point.

CLAIRE. The point being …

ANNA. That it is not to be *believed* …

CLAIRE. Mmm?

ANNA. Our tale is offered, but as a fig leaf of propriety. Not to "explain," but to clothe with the, the …

CLAIRE. Mantle of decency.

ANNA. Yes. That behavior it would be irksome to hear explained.

CLAIRE. You are a Medium.

ANNA. Yes.

CLAIRE. And her *father* …

ANNA. Yes.

CLAIRE. He heard, whilst abroad …

ANNA. Yes.

CLAIRE. Heard, yes, while in the Orient. Of a Fortune-Teller.

ANNA. Mmm. *(Maid enters.)*

MAID. I've come to get me wages.

CLAIRE. One moment, a seer, who could conjure …

ANNA. By means of the jewel.

CLAIRE. Now, there you've lost me.

ANNA. You take the jewel and gaze into it, as into a crystal ball, to determine, do you see? Both the woman's secret ills, and their alleviation.

CLAIRE. … The woman.

ANNA. Yes.

CLAIRE. What woman?

ANNA. Her mother.

CLAIRE. Whose mother?

ANNA. Your friend's mother. My protector's wife. You see, we tell her that's why her father *came.* Not to *betray* his wife, no, but to *aid* her. What is her problem, by the way? Has your friend spoken of it?

CLAIRE. The mother?

ANNA. Yes.

CLAIRE. She is subject, it seems, to those unnamed, vagrant … How did you know she *has* a problem?

ANNA. Her husband has been in the Orient for Seven Years.

CLAIRE. As long as that.

ANNA. He tells me.

CLAIRE. And she lacked the, the …

ANNA. Let us say the capacity for independent *action.*

CLAIRE. *(Pause.)* Makes you think …

ANNA. Well, I'd hardly go *that* far.

MAID. I've come to get me wages.

CLAIRE. And so …

ANNA. So the Husband, do you see, out of Concern.

CLAIRE. Concern, yes.

ANNA. For his *wife* … on his return from Abroad, brought in his wife's jewel, to allow the medium …

CLAIRE. Mmm.

ANNA. … To Divine with it. *(Pause.)*

CLAIRE. Fine. Which leaves only this. How does one explain to the father his daughter's exceptional presence here?

ANNA. Oh, faugh.

CLAIRE. Ah. 'Tis not your ox was gored. Where is your Bible *now?*

ANNA. It's in the morning room.

MAID. I've come to get me wages.

CLAIRE. All right, then, can you think that your protector will continue in his liaison with one *whose Best Friend* had debauched his little girl?

ANNA. Do you suggest he might object?

CLAIRE. You must get out more.

ANNA. *Truly? (Pause.)*

CLAIRE. Yes.

ANNA. What has become of liberality? Of Progressive thought? Of …

CLAIRE. Gone at the slightest hint of difficulty.

ANNA. My oh my.

CLAIRE. Disappeared like an Oil Stock newly invested in by a young Widow.

ANNA. … I ask you.

CLAIRE. … Like a tarsier, at the hint of False Dawn.

ANNA. What is a tarsier?

CLAIRE. It is an East Indian Rodent.

ANNA. *Is* it?

CLAIRE. I believe it is.

ANNA. Noteworthy for its skittishness?

CLAIRE. It is proverbial … but.

ANNA. … live and learn.

CLAIRE. How do we explain to the father the presence here of his little girl?

ANNA. We tell him the selfsame thing.

CLAIRE. To wit:

ANNA. She came here to consult a fortune-teller.

CLAIRE. But he knows you're not a fortune-teller.

ANNA. We tell him *you're* the fortune-teller.

CLAIRE. I'm a fortune-teller, too?

ANNA. Mmm.

CLAIRE. Does that mean I, too, must wear a funny hat?

ANNA. If necessary. *(Pause.)*

CLAIRE. But could such a Byzantine rodomontade restore the girl to me? Could it convince the father?

ANNA. Men live but to be deceived.

CLAIRE. They do?

ANNA. Well, what have I done but deceive him? My protector loves me. He requires my *aid*. How to continue with me when all the world conspires to the contrary. We will mint for him his excuse. And our poor simpering effort will, once again, conquer all. *(Pause.)*

CLAIRE. I have underestimated you.

ANNA. I'm quite aware of it. Oh, my word, in fine: we shall have a *séance*. Eh? Eh?

CLAIRE. A Séance.

ANNA. At Which Séance, I, Madame de …

CLAIRE. Mmm.

MAID. Miss …

ANNA. Yes, shut up one moment, will you…? Will put all …

MAID. Miss …

ANNA. Will put all aright.

CLAIRE. A Séance.

ANNA. At which:

CLAIRE. At which, amidst both the Mumbo and the Jumbo …

ANNA. Mmm.

CLAIRE. You divine …

ANNA. Yes.

CLAIRE. By means of the Jewel …

ANNA. *(Pause.)* But what do we know, what can we adduce or invent of the clairvoyant?

MAID. Miss …

CLAIRE. Shut up for a moment, will you?

MAID. It's a monkey.

CLAIRE. How, at this séance, shall we convince each, of our aforementioned supernormal powers?

ANNA. We shall present them with, with circumstantial facts of their previous lives. *(Pause.)*

CLAIRE. The man was seven years in India.

ANNA. What do we know of India…? *(Pause.)*

CLAIRE. Ah, well …

ANNA. *How* I wish I read …

CLAIRE. *India … (Pause.)*

ANNA. … the, the, the …

CLAIRE. *"India"* …

ANNA. India is possessed of … Or, at the risk of *Pedantry:*

CLAIRE. Please:

ANNA. India is Bounded on the North by …

MAID. It's a monkey.

CLAIRE. Have you not, lacking sufficient awe, that sense of fitness to stand mute before your betters?

MAID. Mum?

CLAIRE. Go away or we shall have a policeman in to shoot you and stick your head on a pike.

MAID. Begging your pardon. It's a monkey.

ANNA. What's a monkey?

MAID. A tarsier. My dad had one in Bengal.

CLAIRE. In Bengal?

MAID. Yuh.

ANNA. Bengal. In India.

MAID. That's right.

ANNA. And did he, as one would assume, regale you with tales of that dark, unknowable land?

MAID. Yes, miss.

ANNA. *(To Claire.)* Write to invite them to our séance.

CLAIRE. … But, but, how …

ANNA. We shall deluge them with, folk, folk wisdom.

CLAIRE. Folk wisdom…?

ANNA. Women's Wisdom, do you see? The Sayings of the Auld Grandmarm.

CLAIRE. The trash the slavey's grandma gibbered.

ANNA. Let it *extract* us from our difficulties. I shall adopt it as that axiom which rules my life. *Molly:*

MAID. I suppose it's bootless to beg for a character.

ANNA. I …

MAID. Just give me me wages.

ANNA. Molly, dear…?

MAID. Did ye want to count the Silver?

ANNA. How *Colorful…!*

MAID. For I've got to look out for meself, you know, for when you turn on me.

ANNA. As if we could distrust you! How I *love* that Earthy Humor.

CLAIRE. Earthy Humor, yes.

ANNA. So …

CLAIRE. Close to the soil. Your mistress would opine perhaps she's been too hasty.

MAID. Too hasty …

ANNA. Yes. I …

CLAIRE. She withdraws the Edict …

MAID. The edict.

CLAIRE. The, the Ukase … the …

47

ANNA. I take back what I said.

CLAIRE. And she *hopes*. That you will see fit to remain in …

ANNA. In my *Service*. *(Pause.)*

MAID. Yeh want me to stay.

CLAIRE. We want you to help us plan a sort of party.

MAID. Waal, I don't know.

ANNA. What don't you know?

MAID. … After th' things you've said …

CLAIRE. Oh, bullshit. Sit down, or we'll throw you in the streets to starve, pox-ridden and pregnant.

ANNA. Nora, oblige us. Please tell us about your grandmother.

MAID. Yes, mum.

ANNA. *(To Claire.)* You see? You see how it profits? One must keep a civil tongue in one's mouth.

CLAIRE. Mmm.

ANNA. … It need not be one's own.

CLAIRE. Well — ain't *you* wicked …

Scene 2

Late. Anna and Claire in vaguely Middle Eastern Garb. Claire goes to examine herself in a mirror.

CLAIRE. The couture of the paranormal does not well withstand the gaze of day.

ANNA. Like that of the boudoir.

CLAIRE. Pray do not taunt me.

ANNA. Quite right. *(Pause.)*

CLAIRE. I feel I'd like to climb beneath some lavishly appointed rock.

ANNA. It is the waiting galls one.

CLAIRE. Is it?

ANNA. Ah, yes, we suffer for our sins, we suffer for them.

CLAIRE. But not before we have made *others* suffer for them.

ANNA. You still indict me for our dilemma?

CLAIRE. I find myself hoping to lure back my love with a funny hat.

ANNA. Is that not woman's lot?

CLAIRE. How ill philosophy becomes you.

ANNA. They will respond.

CLAIRE. I cannot think so. Oh, I am other than well.

ANNA. Do you know. I have noticed. In the midst of this or that upheaval, that at times, the spirit is relieved by the simple increase of *bulk* in the diet. *(Pause.)*

CLAIRE. What *is* bulk?

ANNA. *Bulk,* and I ask your pardon in advance …

CLAIRE. … Please.

ANNA. … Is that which tends toward the cleansing of, I believe, the *colon,* or whatever the … the … *(Pause.)*

CLAIRE. … I never could abide "learning," do you know …

ANNA. Mmm.

CLAIRE. … Always seemed so "pushy."

ANNA. Yes. Down through the ages, it is the historic tool of the Social Climber.

CLAIRE. Are my seams straight?

ANNA. Euclidean. *(The maid enters. All stand.)* Is the room prepared?

MAID. All prepared, mum …

ANNA. Report.

MAID. We got the draperies drawn, the table moved, the chairs all thronged together so the people's knees will touch …

ANNA. The candles…?

MAID. I've lit 'em.

ANNA. Did you not say … did you not say … We must wait till the incantation?

CLAIRE. Isn't that what your Auld Gran said?

ANNA. … Were we not *told* … we must *wait* till the *incantation* …

CLAIRE. Why have you lit the candles?

MAID. Well, the sun's goin' down. *(Pause.)* Where's your guests?

ANNA. Withdraw until you're called. *(Maid exits.)*

CLAIRE. They will not come. They will not respond. We shall be left two foolish old women, trusting to chemistry and candlelight.

ANNA. Be strong.

CLAIRE. Easy for you.

ANNA. If my protector withdraws his support, I am reduced to poverty, but do you see me complain?

CLAIRE. I could compass the girl's waist with my two small hands. But perhaps I grow too technical.

ANNA. Oh God oh God oh God of Hosts, how we are Reduced ... how the Shadow of Poverty ... How *Stress* ...

CLAIRE. What is Of Hosts?

ANNA. It connotes "of Many."

CLAIRE. *Truly...?*

ANNA. Why do you dismiss the comfort of such sacred and archaic language?

CLAIRE. I was brought up in a barn. *(Maid reenters.)*

ANNA. *(To maid.)* What?

MAID. I'm worried, mum.

ANNA. No need to worry. For men live to be deceived. They would rather be deceived than sated. We shall prevail.

MAID. That ain't what worries me.

CLAIRE. What worries you?

MAID. What if I have a child?

CLAIRE. One waits until the colder months, and exposes them in a tree.

ANNA. Off you go! *(Maid exits. Pause.)* May I ask you, do you never feel that you've missed something?

CLAIRE. What would that be?

ANNA. Motherhood.

CLAIRE. Were I to say that the joys of conception, parturition, and lactation had been vouchsafed to me I would tell a lie.

ANNA. Yes. But certain women profit from it.

CLAIRE. In what way?

ANNA. They, they have *children*.

CLAIRE. Apart from that.

ANNA. No. I take your point.

MAID. *(Reentering.)* We ain't got no new candles. *(Pause.)*

CLAIRE. Isn't this always the way.

ANNA. Run quick and get them. Hurry. Go. *(Maid exits.)*

CLAIRE. They have abandoned us. What time is it? They will not come.

ANNA. They will come.

CLAIRE. What will make them come?

ANNA. We shall dispatch a second note.

CLAIRE. A second note?

ANNA. *(To maid, calling after her.)* Send for a messenger.

CLAIRE. And how will this second note be more effective than the first?

ANNA. WE SHALL INVITE THE WIFE!

CLAIRE. … The wife…?

ANNA. How blind I have been. *If* we are soothsayers. As we are. *If* we possess the power to alleviate pain, to, to cure her vapors, to …

CLAIRE. … Yes…?

ANNA. Then let us *cure* the wife! She is the cornerstone! With her endorsement, both the man and the girl are licensed to frequent our home. How *blind* I have been. *(She writes.)* "Madame de blah blah, to whom the future and the past are one, awaits to set your mind at rest. Having divined and prognosticated by the means of *your jewel* … " Ha ha ha ha ha. "And having, at length, diagnosed the cause of your discomfort, she invites you."

CLAIRE. She will not come.

ANNA. She *will* come, and let her call it "Doubt" or "Indignation," let her call it what she will, she must succumb to her curiosity … It is the weakness of the sex. *(Doorbell. Maid passes through.)* Who is it?

MAID. A messenger.

ANNA. … Arrived so soon? Bid him attend a moment … "And to perfect, for you, through the accumulation and dispersal of tea leaves, the lessons of the crystal ball, and the application of exotic herbs." (Resist *that* if you can. She cannot. For women are …)

CLAIRE. … Pray do not say what we are. I know too well what we are …

ANNA. Then you know the wife must come. I've sussed out her fulcrum, it is *Curiosity,* and we have her on the hip. I bet you a new Hat. *(Continues writing.)* "Et *cetera,* to remove those noxious ethereal influences we have found surround you. And restore your spirits and your soul. In the name of various gods, I remain … " *(Maid reenters with a letter. Anna hands the maid the note.)* Give the messenger this. Thank him for his prompt response.

MAID. For what response?

ANNA. To our summons.

MAID. What summons, mum?

ANNA. We summoned him to take a letter.

MAID. No, mum. He *brought* a letter. *(Pause.)* He *brought* a letter. *(She holds out a letter. Claire takes the letter. Opens it. Maid exits.)*

CLAIRE. *(Reads.)* Who is Rehab the Harlot?

ANNA. I believe it is for me.

CLAIRE. Will you hear your fate?

ANNA. I am prepared. *(Reads.)* It is from his attorney. They have decamped. The entire family. He will ... he has, yes, he has terminated the, the "consultation fees," which, of late, it has been his use to pay me.

CLAIRE. ... He no longer desires to consult with you ...

ANNA. ... And he requires the immediate return of his wife's necklace, which had somehow found its accidental way into my possession.

CLAIRE. ... He wants his sparkler back ...

ANNA. ... Absent which ... legal remedies, criminal proceedings, bailiff, theft ... Jail ...

CLAIRE. Oh, dear.

ANNA. ... And he will send an emissary to collect the Jewel.

CLAIRE. *(Takes the letter.)* And pop goes the entire weasel. *(Pause.)*

ANNA. I fear I was mistaken in his steadfastness. *(Pause.)*

CLAIRE. You must keep it, of course.

ANNA. Keep?

CLAIRE. The Jewel.

ANNA. The Jewel. I cannot.

CLAIRE. You must.

ANNA. How can I?

CLAIRE. He gave it to you.

ANNA. It was not his to give.

CLAIRE. Are all our possessions, and all our joys, but loaned on *sufferance,* and subject to the whim of men? He's broke his promise. He's deceived you. He's had the use of your body, and he paid for it with stolen goods. For God's sake keep the necklace.

ANNA. You are *distraught.*

CLAIRE. Have I not cause?

MAID. *(Reentering.)* I'm goin' for the candles, mum.

ANNA. What?

MAID. I'm goin' for th' …

CLAIRE. I don't think we'll require them. *(Pause.)* I doubt we'd want to pay for them. *(Maid exits.)*

ANNA. Well, are we worse off than we were before?

CLAIRE. What a dreary standard by which to gauge one's life.

ANNA. What choice have we but to take heart?

CLAIRE. Are you not, then, chilled by the spectre of poverty?

ANNA. … By poverty?

CLAIRE. Yes.

ANNA. Doth not the Bible teach us to leave ungleaned the corners of our fields?

CLAIRE. I have no idea.

ANNA. I assure you.

CLAIRE. And what might that mean?

ANNA. That the urge, at the risk of tendentiousness …

CLAIRE. … Please.

ANNA. To Consume All.

CLAIRE. Yes, *I* get ya …

ANNA. Oh good. *(Pause.)* And, and …

CLAIRE. … Yes?

ANNA. Might we not then deduce … then, that *true* happiness might lie … not in obtaining the, the object of one's …

CLAIRE. … Lust.

ANNA. If you will, but, in being *free* of it? Would *that* not be joy? *(Pause.)*

CLAIRE. *No. (Pause.)*

ANNA. Oh.

CLAIRE. But thank you for asking.

ANNA. Look here: if we have enough to eat, suitably cut raiment, and shelter from the storm, what do we care?

CLAIRE. You are too good.

ANNA. Not at all. I'm merely practical.

CLAIRE. I have lost her. And with her, the last good instant of my youth.

ANNA. Oh, dear …

CLAIRE. No, it all went pear-shaped.

ANNA. What went all pear-shaped?

CLAIRE. My life.

ANNA. Your life, eh?

CLAIRE. Which once shone so promising.

ANNA. So many things are more amusing in Prospect, don't you find, than ...

CLAIRE. Than in Actuality?

ANNA. Yes,

CLAIRE. No, I do not.

ANNA. Mmm.

CLAIRE. But I treasure your intention to amuse me.

ANNA. *Do* you?

CLAIRE. Quite diverting.

MAID. *(Entering.)* Mum.

ANNA. No, but may one not.

MAID. Mum.

ANNA. One moment, Make that Leap. That, that Act of Renunciation which ...

MAID. Mum.

ANNA. ... Shut up. And, and may we not seek that, that ...

MAID. Mum.

ANNA. One moment, that, that State of Grace, that ...

CLAIRE. I don't think so ...

ANNA. Of, of *acceptance,* yes, if it is offered. Yes, and I think it is, constantly ...

MAID. Mum.

ANNA. One moment. As at a Perfect Inn, or *hostel.*

MAID. Mum. Mum! I just remembered. The cook said you could kiss her arse til Michelmas! *(Pause.)*

ANNA. Thank you. *(Maid exits.)* At a Perfect *Inn,* or *hostel,* I say, waiting, welcoming the legitimately weary.

CLAIRE. ... No.

ANNA. Yes. Ministering to the sore travelers as they trod that way, do you see, they must trod in any case.

CLAIRE. Yes. That would be no end of jolly. Oh, Age, Age, Dreadful Age.

ANNA. As long as, as long as one has not "done evil" ... *(Pause.)*

CLAIRE. ... Done evil?

ANNA. Yes. Caused *pain,* or ...

CLAIRE. ... And, indeed, I have gained nothing and have caused *you* pain.

ANNA. Yes, some, perhaps, but ...

CLAIRE. *That* is a sin ...

ANNA. No, no, a *slip,* perhaps, done in exuberance. But not a true Error ...

CLAIRE. Then what would be example of true error?

ANNA. ... Writing in purple *ink,* or ...

CLAIRE. ... You are too good to live.

ANNA. Is that so?

CLAIRE. I regret that I have enmeshed you in my cabal of loss.

ANNA. Oh pray, do not descend to the literary. *(Pause.) Are* we so badly off? Could we not strive to exist on my income?

CLAIRE. Indeed, how...?

ANNA. Do they not say two can live as cheap as one?

CLAIRE. No doubt. The world is full of fools and if one listens long enough, one may hear damn near anything.

ANNA. But if we curtailed our expenditures, could we not sustain ourselves, say, in the country?

CLAIRE. In the country! You, who, self-confessed, can neither hum nor fart. *(Pause.)* Hum nor fart. *(Pause.)* Fart nor hum. *(Pause.)*

ANNA. "Farm nor hunt"?

CLAIRE. Precisely. What would we do in the country? Sit and pray for dissolution. Like goldfish. Fit only to sicken and die. *(Pause.)*

ANNA. ... I *can* hum, you know.

CLAIRE. Can you indeed?

ANNA. I could *always* hum. I could not *"whistle."* This is not the first time you've confused them. How affective are the very foibles of those close to us? I think that it is charming. What do you think? *(Pause.)* Is it charming?

CLAIRE. It is charming if you are charmed by it. *(Pause.)*

ANNA. Why do you reject those niceties of speech and conduct nature has contrived to even our rough way?

CLAIRE. I have ruint what I touched.

ANNA. ... Claire ...

CLAIRE. Perhaps, as has no doubt been observed before, we human beings are but a plague upon the rocks or plants ... *(Pause.)* Perhaps I am small potatoes. Perhaps I am not potatoes at all.

ANNA. Oh, my dear, you must have loved her.

CLAIRE. I *do* love her.

ANNA. Well. You, you will have her In Retrospect.

CLAIRE. In retrospect?

ANNA. As, do you see, as the *vision* of a flame. Which persists. After the flame is gone.

CLAIRE. No, I don't get you.

ANNA. When you blow the candle out.

CLAIRE. The flame lasts?

ANNA. The vision. The vision of the flame.

CLAIRE. ... Oh, God ... no. Do not look on me. Time drags on. And each day I spin Gold into flax.

ANNA. My dear, could we not intuit, in this Reversal, the, the operations of a Greater Hand?

CLAIRE. A Greater Hand?

ANNA. A Brake, or Governor, upon ...

CLAIRE. A "brake" ...

ANNA. Both our, I believe it. Happiness and Folly.

CLAIRE. If I could but believe ...

ANNA. But the point is not to believe but to decide.

CLAIRE. Oh, my dear. You always were too good for me. God bless you in your naiveté. And when you reminisce, forgive me.

ANNA. When I reminisce...? *(Pause.)*

CLAIRE. You understand that my presence here would be a drain upon both your emotions and your treasury. *(Pause.)* I have spoiled your establishment and traduced your affections. Better for us both to part.

ANNA. *(Pause.)* Oh.

CLAIRE. I know you understand.

ANNA. And I cannot dissuade you?

CLAIRE. I fear you cannot.

ANNA. *(Pause.)* But ...

CLAIRE. Bless you. Your efforts would be in vain.

ANNA. You once said, you could be happy alone with me in a Garret.

CLAIRE. And once I could. Forgive me.

ANNA. *(Pause.)* I will fetch the jewel. *(Exits.)*

CLAIRE. And I shall, like the dying fox, offer amusement to the county. *(Maid enters.)* All undone by Men.

MAID. Excuse me, mum.

CLAIRE. Undone by Men, I opined. Are you deaf?

MAID. What, mum?

CLAIRE. I made fair to make common cause with you, do you see? You, ravaged and abandoned. Myself done out of my birthright. By Men. *(To maid.)* Where are you rushing to?

MAID. I'm goin' for the candles, mum.

CLAIRE. We don't require them now, do you see? For our schemes have miscarried. *(Pause.)* How odd to've supposed a possible alternative.

MAID. I beg your pardon, mum.

CLAIRE. I said we don't require the candles. *(Pause.)* What?

MAID. I tell a lie.

CLAIRE. Again?

MAID. Yes, mum. An' I must beg your pardon.

CLAIRE. What was the lie?

MAID. I'm goin' to see me fella.

CLAIRE. See yer fellow, is it?

MAID. Yes, mum.

CLAIRE. I thought he'd abandoned you.

MAID. No, mum. He changed his mind.

CLAIRE. Oh, good.

MAID. He just sent word as how he wants to meet me in the park to "discuss" something.

CLAIRE. Whatever would *that* be? Some life-enhancing tender of his "troth," so on?

MAID. I hope so, mum.

CLAIRE. Then of course. Off you go. *(Maid exits.)* Off you go to your Bower of Bliss. Off you go to your sweet narcotic. Two souls resubsumed in oblivion. Off you go. I will stay here. *(Pause. Anna enters.)*

ANNA. Where is the slavey?

CLAIRE. Gone out.

ANNA. When?

CLAIRE. Just now.

ANNA. I have been robbed.

CLAIRE. What can you mean?

ANNA. The jewel is gone.

CLAIRE. Where did you look?

ANNA. Everywhere.

CLAIRE. It cannot be.

ANNA. It is.

CLAIRE. Infamia.

ANNA. I am destroyed.

CLAIRE. The girl took the jewel?

ANNA. She, it must be, and her accomplice.

CLAIRE. "That man."

ANNA. Help me.

CLAIRE. Lord, what is not fleeting, here below?

ANNA. They shall cart me to jail.

CLAIRE. … Anna …

ANNA. What shall I do? I cannot bear rebuke, let alone *incarceration* … They will come with, what are they called? One wears them on one's wrists.

CLAIRE. Manacles.

ANNA. And take me away. I, who have required from life so little …

CLAIRE. My dear …

ANNA. And now, and now …

CLAIRE. We can prevail upon your protector.

ANNA. He has denounced me and decamped.

CLAIRE. The cad.

ANNA. And hidden in that woman's skirts.

CLAIRE. His wife.

ANNA. The Foul Fiend.

CLAIRE. What craven cowards they are.

ANNA. But, as they are, always in possession of the Field, how would they learn Nobility?

CLAIRE. But would he, in *truth,* consign you to jail?

ANNA. Oh, my dear, undoubtedly. He has so much of which he is ashamed.

CLAIRE. As do I.

ANNA. Please?

CLAIRE. I am cause of your misfortune. If I had not brought the child here, does not such a speech occur to you?

ANNA. But: none of us is perfect. Each is not only permitted but required to repent ... And if to repent, then of necessity, to err. It is now my lot to attempt that most profoundly difficult of human tasks.

CLAIRE. To forgive one who has wronged you?

ANNA. No, to pack when rushed. What shall I want in a cell? It is so hard to think on the instant. I'll take your portrait. *(Starts to exit.)*

CLAIRE. Take my portrait?

ANNA. The one in the brown kerseymere. You remember.

CLAIRE. I thought he'd got the nose wrong.

ANNA. How little you know of yourself. *(Starts, again, to exit.)*

CLAIRE. Oh, for God's sake: Pack for two.

ANNA. ... I'm sorry?

CLAIRE. I shall, of course, accompany you.

ANNA. No.

CLAIRE. To the contrary.

ANNA. A touch *Ancien Régime,* don't you think?

CLAIRE. I profoundly hope so.

ANNA. But you could not abide jail.

CLAIRE. What have I to fear?

ANNA. The food, the clothing and the conversation.

CLAIRE. We shall brave them together.

ANNA. Shall we?

CLAIRE. Every circumstance conspires to so instruct me.

ANNA. And do you not find such instruction onerous?

CLAIRE. I do not.

ANNA. How can I thank you?

CLAIRE. Hear my confession.

ANNA. Speak to me.

CLAIRE. I abhor chintz. *(Pause.)*

ANNA. You said that you liked it.

CLAIRE. I spoke in jest.

ANNA. Yes, perhaps I have wronged you, too. *(Doorbell.)* That would be the bailiff.

CLAIRE. Are you prepared?

ANNA. I'll have the girl fetch my wrap.

CLAIRE. The girl is gone.

ANNA. Then I shall fetch my wrap myself.

CLAIRE. Oh God, so it begins. *(Anna exits.)* Oh golly how good

59

it feels to be courageous. I wonder if this feeling's widely known. Enter then, sir, and do your worst. *(Maid enters. Pause.)* Vandal, how dare you return?

MAID. I brought a …

CLAIRE. How do you find the gall?

MAID. I brought …

CLAIRE. You brought, what? A fell request for *Ransom?*

MAID. Miss?

CLAIRE. What business have you here?

MAID. I thought I'd make the tea. *(Pause.)*

CLAIRE. The tea?

MAID. It's teatime.

CLAIRE. Where is your mistress's necklace?

MAID. In the Bible.

CLAIRE. … In the Bible?

MAID. In the morning room. She left it in there, marking her place.

CLAIRE. Did she, indeed?

MAID. She did. She never can remember where she put it.

CLAIRE. … Yes. *(Pause.)*

MAID. I brought you a note.

CLAIRE. A note.

MAID. There's a young lady, gave it to me.

CLAIRE. A young lady?

MAID. In a carriage, waitin' on the corner.

CLAIRE. Give me the note. *(Maid hands her the note. Claire opens it and reads.)*

MAID. She said she ain't got but the one instant she could stay, for yer answer. Though, I must say, she didn't have to be so *snappish*. For, din't I give up me meeting with me feller, just to bring the note in. D'you think she might let me step out this evening, do you think?

CLAIRE. … step out?

MAID. Me mistress, as I had t'forgo me afternoon outing.

CLAIRE. Developing a taste for the Carnal, are we?

MAID. Yes, miss. That's the sad part. Can't help meself.

CLAIRE. Mmm.

MAID. D'you think she would? Let me step out this evening?

CLAIRE. If you *do,* remember to instruct your friend to brush your back off when you get up from the ground.

MAID. We do it up against a tree.

CLAIRE. Isn't that hard on the legs?

MAID. Perhaps. But the view is better.

CLAIRE. What in life is not a compromise?

MAID. Love. *(Pause.)*

CLAIRE. May you find it so.

MAID. The girl can stay just the one minute, and then she'll be gone. *(Pause.)*

CLAIRE. Just the one moment, and then she'll be gone.

MAID. You'll want me to take out your answer? *(Claire stops reading the note.)*

CLAIRE. No, there is no answer.

MAID. Very good, miss. Then I'll make the tea. *(Maid exits. Claire tears the note in half. Anna reenters, carrying a small carpetbag and portrait.)*

CLAIRE. You take so little.

ANNA. I have what I require. Shall we await them in the air?

CLAIRE. Await them…?

ANNA. Yes, the bailiffs.

CLAIRE. … Ah.

ANNA. For it seems I am finished with this house.

CLAIRE. Yes. Let us sit in the park, for I have various things I'd like to say to you.

ANNA. But are you *resigned?* Are you, indeed, resigned to accompany me into Exile?

CLAIRE. Not resigned, but honored.

ANNA. Better than the best of friends.

CLAIRE. And you shall be my preceptor.

ANNA. … My dear? …

CLAIRE. You shall guide me — for you are gifted to move in a world I cannot see. The world you see is not cruel. Possessing neither falsity nor guile. And it shall be my mission to protect you from it.

ANNA. And you are returned to me.

CLAIRE. With all my heart.

ANNA. But will your feelings never change?

CLAIRE. That is not within my gift. But I will never leave you.

Might that do?

ANNA. I am content.

CLAIRE. Then I will count the day a triumph. *(They embrace and exit. The maid reenters, followed immediately by Anna.)*

ANNA. Mary. A gentleman will call for the jewel.

MAID. Yes, mum.

ANNA. It's in the Bible in the morning room. Give it to him.

MAID. Yes, mum.

ANNA. And get a receipt. *(Anna starts to exit. Maid curtseys. Maid holds up a muff.)*

MAID. Miss, your friend's forgot her muff.

ANNA. *(Exiting.)* No, that remains to be seen. *(Exits.)*

End of Play

PROPERTY LIST

Tea service (MAID)
Muff (CLAIRE, MAID)
Jewelry bag (ANNA)
Paper and pen (ANNA)
Letter (MAID)
Small carpetbag and portrait (ANNA)

SOUND EFFECTS

Doorbell
Crash

NEW PLAYS

★ **MONTHS ON END by Craig Pospisil.** In comic scenes, one for each month of the year, we follow the intertwined worlds of a circle of friends and family whose lives are poised between happiness and heartbreak. "…a triumph…these twelve vignettes all form crucial pieces in the eternal puzzle known as human relationships, an area in which the playwright displays an assured knowledge that spans deep sorrow to unbounded happiness." –*Ann Arbor News.* "…rings with emotional truth, humor…[an] endearing contemplation on love…entertaining and satisfying." –*Oakland Press.* [5M, 5W] ISBN: 0-8222-1892-5

★ **GOOD THING by Jessica Goldberg.** Brings us into the households of John and Nancy Roy, forty-something high-school guidance counselors whose marriage has been increasingly on the rocks and Dean and Mary, recent graduates struggling to make their way in life. "…a blend of gritty social drama, poetic humor and unsubtle existential contemplation…" –*Variety.* [3M, 3W] ISBN: 0-8222-1869-0

★ **THE DEAD EYE BOY by Angus MacLachlan.** Having fallen in love at their Narcotics Anonymous meeting, Billy and Shirley-Diane are striving to overcome the past together. But their relationship is complicated by the presence of Sorin, Shirley-Diane's fourteen-year-old son, a damaged reminder of her dark past. "…a grim, insightful portrait of an unmoored family…" –*NY Times.* "MacLachlan's play isn't for the squeamish, but then, tragic stories delivered at such an unrelenting fever pitch rarely are." –*Variety.* [1M, 1W, 1 boy] ISBN: 0-8222-1844-5

★ **[SIC] by Melissa James Gibson.** In adjacent apartments three young, ambitious neighbors come together to discuss, flirt, argue, share their dreams and plan their futures with unequal degrees of deep hopefulness and abject despair. "A work…concerned with the sound and power of language…" –*NY Times.* "…a wonderfully original take on urban friendship and the comedy of manners—a *Design for Living* for our times…" –*NY Observer.* [3M, 2W] ISBN: 0-8222-1872-0

★ **LOOKING FOR NORMAL by Jane Anderson.** Roy and Irma's twenty-five-year marriage is thrown into turmoil when Roy confesses that he is actually a woman trapped in a man's body, forcing the couple to wrestle with the meaning of their marriage and the delicate dynamics of family. "Jane Anderson's bittersweet transgender domestic comedy-drama …is thoughtful and touching and full of wit and wisdom. A real audience pleaser." –*Hollywood Reporter.* [5M, 4W] ISBN: 0-8222-1857-7

★ **ENDPAPERS by Thomas McCormack.** The regal Joshua Maynard, the old and ailing head of a mid-sized, family-owned book-publishing house in New York City, must name a successor. One faction in the house backs a smart, "pragmatic" manager, the other faction a smart, "sensitive" editor and both factions fear what the other's man could do to this house— and to them. "If Kaufman and Hart had undertaken a comedy about the publishing business, they might have written *Endpapers*…a breathlessly fast, funny, and thoughtful comedy …keeps you amused, guessing, and often surprised…profound in its empathy for the paradoxes of human nature." –*NY Magazine.* [7M, 4W] ISBN: 0-8222-1908-5

★ **THE PAVILION by Craig Wright.** By turns poetic and comic, romantic and philosophical, this play asks old lovers to face the consequences of difficult choices made long ago. "The script's greatest strength lies in the genuineness of its feeling." –*Houston Chronicle.* "Wright's perceptive, gently witty writing makes this familiar situation fresh and thoroughly involving." –*Philadelphia Inquirer.* [2M, 1W (flexible casting)] ISBN: 0-8222-1898-4

DRAMATISTS PLAY SERVICE, INC.
440 Park Avenue South, New York, NY 10016 212-683-8960 Fax 212-213-1539
postmaster@dramatists.com www.dramatists.com

NEW PLAYS

★ **YELLOWMAN by Dael Orlandersmith.** A multi-character memory play about an African-American woman who dreams of life beyond the confines of her small-town Southern upbringing and the light-skinned man whose fate is tragically intertwined with hers. Finalist for the Pulitzer Prize. "…prophetic and affirmative…a battle cry for humanity and its possibilities." –*NY Times.* "Both a celebration of young love and a harrowing study of smoldering domestic violence, the play is both heartwarming and ultimately heart-breaking." –*Variety.* [1M, 1W] ISBN: 0-8222-1880-1

★ **THE GUYS by Anne Nelson.** Less than two weeks after the events of September 11th, an editor named Joan comes together with a fire captain to help craft eulogies for firemen lost in the attack. Based on a true story. "Ms. Nelson's play…gives credible and powerful voice to a very specific kind of pain…perhaps the keenest message to emerge from *The Guys* is the assertion that writers—and actors—have a serious role to play in a grieving society." –*NY Times.* [1M, 1W] ISBN: 0-8222-1908-6

★ **HEDWIG AND THE ANGRY INCH by John Cameron Mitchell and Stephen Trask.** The story of "internationally ignored song stylist" Hedwig Schmidt, a fourth-wall smashing East German rock 'n' roll goddess who also happens to be the victim of a botched sex-change operation, which has left her with just "an angry inch." "In the whole long, sorry history of rock musicals, *Hedwig and the Angry Inch* is the first one that truly rocks." –*Rolling Stone.* [1M, 1W (flexible casting)] ISBN: 0-8222-1901-8

★ **BOSTON MARRIAGE by David Mamet.** Set in a drawing room, this droll comedy of errors follows two scheming "women of fashion" as they exchange barbs, taunt their Scottish maid and conspire in pursuit of social and sexual conquests as the Victorian era draws to a close. "Devastatingly funny…exceptionally clever…[Mamet] demonstrates anew his technical virtuosity and flexibility." –*NY Times.* "…[a] marriage of glinting period artifice and contemporary frankness." –*Boston Phoenix.* [3W] ISBN: 0-8222-1944-1

★ **THE LIEUTENANT OF INISHMORE by Martin McDonagh.** On a lonely road on the island of Inishmore, someone killed an IRA enforcer's cat. He'll want to know who when he gets back from a stint of torture and chip-shop bombing in Northern Ireland. He loves his cat more than life itself, and someone is going to pay. "…cunningly constructed, deeply and intensely felt, bitterly blood curdling and breathtakingly funny." –*Sunday Times (London).* "The plot is so sublime, the script so witty and the twist at the end so clever that I was won over…" –*The Stage.* [7M, 1W] ISBN: 0-8222-1934-4

★ **THE DAZZLE by Richard Greenberg.** A pair of early twentieth-century bachelor brothers bury themselves under collectibles and trash in their Harlem mansion in this gorgeous tale of mental collapse. Loosely based on the true story of the Collyer brothers. "…a beautiful, disturbing, shockingly funny and profoundly humane play by a masterful dramatist—a writer fearless in his use of poetic imagery, bitterly acid in his irony and, simultaneously, rapturously romantic and horrifyingly clear eyed in his assessment of life." –*Chicago Sun-Times.* [2M, 1W] ISBN: 0-8222-1915-8

★ **BLUE/ORANGE by Joe Penhall.** In a London psychiatric hospital, an enigmatic patient claims to be the son of an exiled African dictator—a story that becomes unnervingly plausible—in this incendiary tale of race, madness and a Darwinian power struggle at the heart of Britain's deteriorating National Health Service. "Exuberant…Penhall has the gift of making serious points in a comic manner and of conveying moral indignation without preaching." –*Guardian (London).* [3M] ISBN: 0-8222-1935-2

DRAMATISTS PLAY SERVICE, INC.
440 Park Avenue South, New York, NY 10016 212-683-8960 Fax 212-213-1539
postmaster@dramatists.com www.dramatists.com

BOSTON MARRIAGE
by David Mamet

3W

Anna and Claire are two bantering, scheming "women of fashion" who have long lived together on the fringes of upper-class society. Anna has just become the mistress of a wealthy man, from whom she has received an enormous emerald and an income to match. Claire, meanwhile, is infatuated with a respectable young lady and wants to enlist the jealous Anna's help for an assignation. As the two women exchange barbs and take turns taunting Anna's hapless Scottish parlor maid, Claire's young inamorata suddenly appears, setting off a crisis that puts both the valuable emerald and the women's futures at risk. To this wickedly funny comedy, Mamet brings his trademark tart dialogue and impeccable plotting, spiced with Wildean wit.

"Brilliant … One of Mamet's most satisfying and accomplished plays and one of the funniest American comedies in years." **—The New York Post**

"Devastatingly funny … exceptionally clever … demonstrates anew [Mamet's] technical virtuosity and flexibility." **—The New York Times**

"Wickedly, wittily entertaining … What makes the play … such brilliant fun is its marriage of glinting period artifice and contemporary frankness." **—The Boston Phoenix**

"[Mamet's characters] are at each other's throats with a wit akin to characters out of Wilde and a vengeance not unlike those from Pinter, Edward Albee, or Mamet himself." **—The Boston Globe**

Also by David Mamet
THE CRYPTOGRAM
OLEANNA
SHORT PI
and many others

ISBN 0-8222-1944-1

DRAMATISTS PLAY SERVICE, INC.